Jesus said, "Let the little children come to Me, and do not
hinder them, for the kingdom of God belongs to such as
these." (Matthew 19:14 and Mark 10:14)

    The FamilyTime Bible Stories series is dedicated to
Jesus, and to families. It is the hope and prayer of those who
worked on these stories that they would help families grow
closer to God.

    To my own family, Erik, Julia and Daniel.

Anne de Graaf

August 1987

Book 2

Brother
against Brother

Written by Anne de Graaf
Illustrated by José Pérez Montero

FamilyTime Bible Stories

ZONDERVAN

Israel - Brother against Brother

Table of Contents — Genesis 23-41

Summary of Book 2

These stories are taken from the second half of the Book of Genesis. They continue the tale of Abraham and his family, chosen by God to be His special people. Abraham's son, Isaac, finds a wife and together they begin the family which God promised Abraham and Sarah for so many years.

Many events described in this book are about brothers fighting brothers. Jacob and Esau are Isaac's sons. They fight over who will take Isaac's place in the family. Joseph is the son of Jacob, or Israel, as he is later called. His brothers do not like him because he is their father's favorite.

In both cases, God heals the brothers' broken relationships after they have spent many years apart. In Joseph's story, God uses the bad thing which Joseph's brothers do to him and protects them against starving to death. The Lord's blessing on these families turns hatred and jealousy into forgiveness and healing.

At this time, God's chosen people are still wandering in the land promised them by God. They live in tents and raise sheep and goats. The land is not theirs yet. Many hundreds of years after they have moved to Egypt, they will return to these same places where Abraham, Isaac and Jacob live. Only then will they settle in the promised land.

WHERE IS ISAAC'S WIFE?

Mission Impossible

Genesis 23:1-:2, 24:1-:27

Abraham and Sarah lived many years together, raising their son Isaac. When Sarah was 127 years old, she died and Abraham felt empty inside.

One of the ways God helped Abraham get over Sarah's death was through the love he shared with Isaac. The father and son took care of each other.

Abraham noticed Isaac had grown into a young man, tall, straight and clever. He knew it was time for Isaac to have a wife. Abraham wanted Isaac to have as good a wife as Sarah had been for him. She must be a kind woman who would love Isaac and help him follow God.

Abraham called his servant one day and gave him a mission. "I want you to find a wife for Isaac. Go back to my people and choose a woman from there."

The servant loaded up several camels with jewels and silk, which he could give to the woman he might find.

It was a nearly impossible mission. There were so many women. How would he know the right one? What if she did not want to come back with him?

Abraham had said, "An angel will arrive there before you and make sure you are in the right place at the right time."

The servant thought about this and prayed to Abraham's God all during the journey. Finally he arrived by a well in the land where Abraham was born.

He prayed, "O Lord of my master Abraham, You choose the woman You know is right for Isaac. Show me clearly who she is. If I ask her for some water and she says, 'Drink, and I'll water your camels, too,' then I will know she is the one."

The servant sat down by the well and waited. Soon he saw a group of young women coming toward him. Each had a water jar on her shoulder. One girl was slim and walked so gracefully she hardly seemed to carry anything at all.

The servant said a prayer, then went to her. "Please give me a little water from your jar," he asked. This was the test. What would she answer?

"Drink, my lord, and I'll water your camels, too." The servant was so excited he forgot to drink. He asked her what family she came from. She named a family, and it was the same as Abraham's!

The servant knew then this lovely young woman was the one God meant to become Isaac's wife. His mission had not been so impossible, after all, since God had arranged it.

Rebekah

Genesis 24:28-:67

The servant gave the girl a bracelet, then thanked God for leading him to Abraham's relatives.

When she heard the servant's prayer, she picked up her skirts and ran home as fast as she could. "Mother, Father," she called out breathlessly, "there is this man by the well and he has come from very far away. He says he works for our long-lost uncle Abraham and look," she held out her arm. "He gave me this bracelet."

The girl's name was Rebekah. When her brother Laban saw the bracelet he knew a very important man must have sent the servant. He invited the servant to come and stay with them.

The servant told them about Abraham, where he lived and that he had become a rich man. Then he told about Isaac, the special son for whom Abraham and Sarah had waited so long. He told about his prayers that God would lead him to just the right woman.

When Rebekah's family heard this, they shook their heads in amazement. Surely God was very great to make it all happen at just the right time and place.

The servant asked them, "Will you allow Rebekah to come with me and marry Isaac?"

Her family said, "This is from the Lord. Here is Rebekah. Take her and go, as the Lord has directed."

When Abraham's servant heard this he bowed down to the ground and thanked God again. He wanted to leave right away, he was so excited and could not wait to see the look on Isaac's face when he saw Rebekah.

Rebekah's family called her and asked, "Will you go with this man?"

"I will go," she said. Rebekah had never met Isaac. She did not know anything about him except that he worshipped the Lord. She also knew that the Lord had led Abraham's servant to her.

That evening Rebekah and her maids climbed on their camels and started back the way the servant had come. After many days, they finally came within sight of Abraham's tents.

On the day they arrived, Isaac was working in the fields. It was hot and he had been working hard, sweating in the sun. He looked up and saw camels coming toward him. "Who is that beautiful woman there?" he wondered. He walked toward the camels.

At the same time Rebekah looked toward Isaac. "Who is that handsome man?" she asked Abraham's servant.

"That is Isaac." She quickly covered her face with her veil. But her eyes shone when Isaac stopped her camel. Theirs was love at first sight.

Soon Rebekah and Isaac were married. Isaac loved Rebekah very much, and her love for him made Isaac feel better after his mother's death. God had known just the right person to care for Isaac and just the right person to care for Rebekah.

ABRAHAM'S LAST DAYS

Isaac and Rebekah

Genesis 25:1-:11

Abraham's heart was warm with joy when he saw how much Isaac loved Rebekah. He felt it was time for Isaac to take over as head of the family. "Now I can die and be with the Lord and see my Sarah again," he thought.

After a long life which had lasted 175 years, Abraham died. Isaac buried him next to Sarah's grave.

After Abraham died, Isaac hurt inside because he missed his father so much.

Sometimes he cried, remembering how much Abraham and Sarah had loved him and wanted him. At those times he was especially thankful for his beautiful Rebekah. She said tender words to him and made him smile when he did not want to.

As the years went by, Isaac learned to listen for God's voice. He learned to trust in what God said. Year followed year, and the only difference between them were the growing numbers of sheep, cattle and camels Isaac owned. He became a rich man.

Rebekah prayed for her husband every day, that he would grow closer and closer to God. But there was one more thing she prayed for every day. And that was for a child. Rebekah and Isaac, just like Sarah and Abraham, did not have any children in the first years of their marriage.

They had plenty to eat, many servants and all the desert to roam in, but no children. Nonetheless, they trusted the Lord to provide the family He had promised them. So they waited.

TWO SONS WHO COULD NOT SHARE

Twin Brothers

Genesis 25:19-:26

Isaac and Rebekah tried to obey God in whatever they did. They asked God's help whenever they made decisions about where to live, how to judge right from wrong, and forgiving people who were mean to them. With God's help, they lived good lives.

But as the years went by they still did not have a little girl or boy. Rebekah and Isaac waited and waited. Until finally, Isaac prayed to God, asking Him to make it possible for a baby to grow inside Rebekah and be born.

A short time later, God answered Isaac's prayer, but not in the way they expected. There was not one baby growing inside Rebekah, but two! Twin babies grew inside Rebekah's tummy.

The babies got bigger and bigger. When it was almost time for them to be born, Rebekah could often feel their little feet pushing against her. Isaac liked to put his hand on her and feel the babies moving inside.

One night, Rebekah woke up suddenly. The babies had been kicking and hitting each other so hard, she hurt inside. She prayed to God, "Oh, Lord, what is happening? Are my babies all right? If I hurt when they push and shove, they must hurt, too. Why is this happening?"

God answered her, "The two boys you carry will someday be fathers of whole nations. One people will be stronger than the other. And the older son will do what the younger tells him."

The time finally came for Rebekah to have her babies. When they were born, the eldest, the first one to come out, was red, and his whole little body was covered with hair. He was named Esau, which meant "Hairy." A few minutes later, his brother came out of Rebekah.

His tiny hand was holding onto Esau's foot. So his parents named him Jacob, which meant "He Grabs the Heel."

An Expensive Breakfast

Genesis 25:27-:34

Many years passed and the boys grew up. They were both good at doing different things. Jacob was a quiet person, often helping at home and talking to his parents. Esau could hunt and catch wild animals. Their father's favorite food was meat from wild animals, and he was glad that Esau could hunt so well.

One day, when Jacob was cooking a stew, Esau came back from hunting. He was very hungry. Esau had not eaten anything the whole day.

"Quick, give me some of that stew!" he said to Jacob. "I'm so hungry I could eat a camel." Esau, sat down on the other side of the fire from Jacob. He could hardly wait for Jacob to pour the stew into a bowl. He wanted to scoop it out of the pot with his own two hands.

Jacob listened to his older brother talk about how hungry he was, and he thought of a plan. Jacob knew he had everything. His parents loved him, he had plenty to eat, and he was healthy. Yet there was one more thing Jacob wanted, and that was Esau's birthright.

Because Esau was the eldest, Esau had a right to receive all of Isaac's riches and animals and servants, once Isaac died, just as Isaac had received these things from Abraham, when Abraham died. This right was called Esau's birthright. Jacob did not like this. He wanted to be the eldest. He wished for it so much, he got angry sometimes. "Why does hairy, old Esau have to be the eldest?" he wondered.

So Jacob made a deal with Esau. "If you're really hungry," Jacob said, "if you're really, really hungry, then sell me your birthright and I'll give you some stew."

Esau hardly heard what his little brother was mumbling about. Esau was hungry, he thought his stomach had shrivelled up and died. He did not care what he had to do, he wanted food. "Yes, all right, whatever you say. Now give me some stew now!"

"Swear to it first," Jacob said. So Esau swore an oath to him, selling his birthright to Jacob.

Jacob gave Esau his bread and stew. After Esau finished eating, he felt foolish for having traded something so important for a bowl of stew. He felt like Jacob had tricked him. Still, what was done was done. So he stood up and left, without saying a word to Jacob.

Rebekah Is Cunning

Genesis 27:1-:40

As the two brothers grew older, Jacob became Rebekah's favorite son. She loved Esau, too, but for Jacob, she wanted only the very best.

When Isaac grew into an old man, he could no longer see and spent most of his time in bed. One day, Isaac called Esau to him. "My son, because you are the eldest, I want to give you the blessing Abraham gave me. First, though, go out hunting and cook some tasty meat for me. Then I will give you your blessing."

Rebekah had overheard what Isaac said to Esau. After Esau left, she called Jacob and said, "Your father is about to give Esau his blessing. I want you to have that. Go and kill two of our best goats. I will fix them just the way Isaac likes his meat. Then you can bring it in to him and you will get his blessing instead."

Jacob knew the plan was not right, yet he did as he was told. When the food was ready, Rebekah glued goat fur to Jacob's neck and arms and hands so his skin would feel like Esau's hairy skin.

Jacob went into his father's room.

"Were you so fast, my son?" Isaac asked.

"Yes, Father."

"But you sound like Jacob. Come here," Isaac said. Jacob went to the bedside of his blind father. Isaac ran his hands over Jacob and felt the hair of the goatskin. "You feel like Esau, though," he said.

Then Isaac tasted the food Jacob gave him. "Ah," he said. There was one last test, though. "Come here and kiss me, my son," Isaac said.

Rebekah had dressed Jacob in Esau's clothes. When Jacob bent over Isaac and Isaac smelled him, Isaac said, "Ah, you smell like the fields where you have been hunting. You are indeed Esau. So here is your blessing."

A blessing was a very special thing. Isaac knew God was listening when he asked God to make his son rich. He prayed that other people, including his brother, would serve this son. He asked God to bless all the people who were good to his son, and curse those who were mean. When Isaac finished praying, Jacob left the room.

A little later Esau returned from his hunting trip! He rushed into his father's room with the food he had fixed, but Isaac said, "Why have you come back a second time?"

"This is my first time," Esau said.

Isaac sighed. "That must have been Jacob

then. Esau, your brother has stolen your blessing."

Esau was very, very angry. "Isn't there any more blessing for me?" he cried.

All Isaac could say was Esau would have to serve Jacob. Esau would be a fighter, but someday, he would be free from his brother who had cheated him. This was not what Esau wanted to hear. He stomped out of his father's bedroom, too angry to think straight.

A Family Is Divided

Genesis 27:41-28:9

Esau could not believe his little brother had tricked him a second time. First, Jacob had taken his birthright, all the riches he would have inherited once Isaac died. Then Jacob had stolen his blessing, God's protection for the future. Esau was so angry, he decided to kill his brother.

Rebekah found out about Esau's plan and warned Jacob. "You will have to go and live with my brother, Laban. His home is very, very far away but if you stay there, Esau may forget how angry he is with you," she said.

There was nothing Isaac could do about

Jacob and Esau. Jacob was the one with God's blessing and Isaac could not take it back. So he called Jacob to him and taught him about God's promises to Abraham for their family.

Isaac said someday God would give them a beautiful land and make them into a large group of people, with many children, as many as the stars in the sky. "But you cannot marry any of the women from around here," Isaac told him. "Go back to your mother's family and marry one of Laban's daughters. Then bring her here and may God bless you and your family."

Jacob listened to his parents' advice. He packed his things, quickly said goodbye, then disappeared into the desert.

By the time Esau heard about it, Jacob was long gone. He knew it was useless to try and follow. So Esau stayed with his parents, taking care of them in their old age.

He may not have had his father's blessing, and he may have been foolish enough to trade his birthright for a bowl of stew, but Esau knew it was an honor to take care of his parents as they grew older. Esau would keep the family strong until Jacob returned.

THE STORY OF JACOB

The Faraway Family

Genesis 28:10-29:14

Jacob's journey would be a long one. He was running away from Esau, and very much afraid that Esau might try to catch up with him. Jacob was more than a little nervous about the trip. He hoped he would have enough food and water. On his first night alone in the desert, Jacob had a strange dream.

Jacob saw a ladder rise up high into the sky. Angels climbed the ladder, going up and down. And at the very top, stood the Lord.

God said, "I am the Lord, the God of your grandfather, Abraham, and of your father, Isaac. I will give you and all your children the very land where you sleep now. There will be so many in your family, it will number more than all the little pieces of dust on the Earth. Everyone on Earth will be blessed because of you and your family. I am with you and will take care of you wherever you go. I will make sure you come back to this land."

When Jacob woke up, he was amazed by his dream. It was so real! God had been right there, just above him. Jacob looked up, but saw only an endless blanket of stars, stretching from horizon to horizon. "This must be a very special place. The Lord is here," he thought to himself. Jacob called the place Bethel.

After many days of travelling, Jacob arrived at a well where shepherds often brought their sheep to drink. A huge stone lay over the well.

When Jacob asked the shepherds if they had ever heard of Laban, they said yes, they had. They pointed to a young woman who was bringing her sheep in with the rest. "Look," said the shepherds, "that girl is Rachel, she is Laban's daughter."

Jacob could hardly believe his ears. He knew his long journey must be almost over.

Then he asked the shepherds why they didn't roll back the stone so the sheep could drink. "Oh no, it is too heavy. We always wait until all the shepherds are here so we can do it together," they said. So Jacob picked up the heavy stone all by himself. With a mighty heave, he pushed it off.

Then he turned to Rachel, who had been watching him. He was so relieved to see a member of the family for whom he had walked so very far, he kissed her. "I am Jacob, your cousin," he said.

Rebekah ran back to her father and told him. Laban went out to the well and hugged Jacob, welcoming him. Laban brought him home and the whole family was hugging and kissing and crying, everyone was so happy to see the son of Rebekah, who had left so many, many years ago.

The Cheater Gets Cheated

Genesis 29:14-29:30

Jacob told Laban about his parents and what had happened during the many years since Rebekah had left her home as a young girl. "And so, my father said I must come here to find a wife because the tribes near us do not worship the one true God," Jacob said.

Laban nodded, but he was not paying much attention. Laban was greedy and selfish. He had two daughters and Jacob was looking for a wife. "All right, Jacob," Laban said. "We would love to have you stay with us. If you work for us, though, surely there is something you want in return."

"Oh yes, Uncle," said Jacob. He looked across the room at Rachel. Her eyes were large and soft, with long lashes. She looked at Jacob, then looked down, and Jacob knew he had found his bride. Already he felt his love for Rachel growing. "Yes, Uncle, I want to marry Rachel. And I will work seven years for you as payment."

"Fine, fine. She might as well marry you as anyone else. Yes, do stay here and work for me then," Laban agreed. Laban was thinking of an evil plan. While Rachel was lovely to look at, her older sister, Leah, was not. Nor could she see very well. Laban rubbed his hands together. He knew a way to trick Jacob.

Jacob worked hard for seven years. Every morning he watched the lovely Rachel walk toward the pastures with her sheep. When she waved at him his heart soared to the hills with her. He hardly noticed the seven years go by, he was so much in love. "Rachel, my Rachel," he sang to himself as he worked in the fields.

When the time was up, Jacob went to Laban and said, "I have worked for you seven years. Now I want to marry Rachel."

But Laban was mean. The time had come for him to play his trick on Jacob. On the wedding night it was dark and the bride was wrapped in veils. It was not until the morning after the wedding that Jacob saw who lay in bed next to him. It was not the beautiful Rachel. No! It was Leah.

"Laban, you tricked me!" Jacob stormed into Laban's tent. As he said the words, he remembered how he, too, had once tricked his brother Esau. He had tricked Esau out of both his birthright and blessing. Now he knew what it felt like to be tricked. Jacob did not think it felt very good. "Laban, give me Rachel!" he demanded.

"Now calm down, calm down," Laban said. "It is not our custom to let the younger daughter marry before the eldest. You will marry Rachel. But since you have already had Leah as your wife you must work another seven years as payment for Rachel," Laban said.

The next week Jacob finally married Rachel. But at the same time, he began to work yet another seven years for Laban.

Time to Go Home

Genesis 29:31-31:55

The second seven years during which Jacob worked for Laban seemed to last forever. But God had not forgotten Jacob, and He blessed everything Jacob did, even giving him many children.

But all the children belonged to Leah. While she had had six children, Rachel had none. After several years and praying to God over and over again, Rachel finally did have a son, though. She named him Joseph and he was a very special little boy.

The day came when little Joseph's father, Jacob, told Laban, "I have worked long and hard for you. Now let me go back to my own family."

"Oh no," thought Laban, "I need Jacob. He is far too good a worker for me to lose."

Laban said, "Name your wage, Jacob. Stay with me and I will pay you whatever you want."

Jacob asked God what he should do. God told him to ask for all the dark, speckled, striped or spotted sheep and goats in Laban's flock. Jacob did so and Laban agreed.

More years went by, and God blessed Jacob's sheep and goats. They became stronger and more plentiful than Laban's and Laban became jealous.

Jacob could tell his uncle did not like him anymore, and he was tired of working for Laban. So for the second time, Jacob decided it was finally time to go home. Twenty years had passed since he had left home and he wanted to see his parents again. Jacob told his wives to organize the children, all the sheep and goats that were his, the servants and tents. They loaded the camels and left...without telling Laban.

When Laban heard Jacob was gone, he became very angry. He ran after Jacob. "What have you done, stealing my daughters and grandchildren away?" he yelled up at Jacob, who sat on his camel.

"Laban, I have worked for you twenty years. Surely I have earned the right to go home. I have never cheated you. We stole nothing from you. Now let us make peace and promise never to harm each other." Laban agreed. Then he kissed Leah and Rachel and all his grandchildren and went back home.

Jacob started the long journey back to Isaac and Rebekah, not knowing what home would be like after twenty years. He was a rich man, but he still felt uneasy about the way he had tricked Esau. He wondered how his brother felt about him.

The Wrestling Match and Jacob's New Name

Genesis 32:1-:30

As Jacob came closer and closer to home, he felt more and more nervous about Esau. Would his brother still be angry? Just to be on the safe side, Jacob sent messengers to Esau. They were to tell Esau that Jacob was very rich, finally coming home and that he wanted to be friends.

When the messengers returned, they said

Esau was coming to meet Jacob, and that he was bringing four hundred men with him!

"Oh no!" thought Jacob. "Esau is coming to destroy me."

He prayed, "Oh Lord, You have been so very good to me. I left home with nothing, but now I return with more than I know what to do with. Please save me from Esau. Let no harm come to the mothers and children. Please Lord," Jacob pleaded with God.

He felt very small that night, the night before Esau arrived. It was to become a night full of surprises, though, a night Jacob would never forget.

As Jacob stood alone under the stars, worrying and praying, a Man came from out of the desert. It was dark and Jacob could not see who the Man was. It was not Esau. Whoever it was, the Man was very strong and He wrestled with Jacob.

All night long the two grabbed and grappled, rolling in the sand, over and over again, panting and heaving. But neither seemed to win. They were of equal strength. Then the Stranger touched the bones in Jacob's leg, causing one bone to come loose. Jacob hurt from the loose bone.

The strange Man said, "Let Me go, it will soon be sunrise."

Then Jacob knew who He was. "This is no ordinary man," Jacob thought. "It is either an angel or...could it be? It is the Lord God Himself."

"What is your name?" the Stranger asked.

"Jacob."

"No, you are no longer Jacob. Your new name is Israel, because you have struggled with God and with men, and you have won," the Stranger said.

"And what is Your name, please?" Jacob said.

"Why should you ask?" the Stranger said, not answering. Then He blessed Jacob, as Jacob lay panting in the desert dust and the sun started its climb over the horizon.

Suddenly, the Stranger was gone and Jacob knew he had seen God face to face. He knew he was lucky to still be alive. The sky shone pink and gold as Jacob limped back to camp. Before he arrived, though, he saw a crowd of men coming toward him.

Jacob Sees Esau Again

Genesis 33:1-:20

When Jacob saw the crowd, he called Rachel and Leah and all his children. He lined them up, with Rachel and Joseph coming last. Then he went to the head of the line and limped out to meet Esau. He limped because he still hurt from having stayed up all night, wrestling with the Lord.

When he met Esau, Jacob bowed down to the ground seven times. Although afraid, Jacob was excited and honored to see his older brother again. He prayed Esau would forgive him.

Jacob's prayers were answered! For when Esau saw Jacob, he jumped off his camel, gathered his robes up and ran straight for Jacob. Esau's four hundred men watched and Jacob's wives and children watched.

The two men hugged each other and cried and hugged some more. Oh, they were glad to be back together again! All was forgiven. What mattered was they were brothers and the long twenty years apart were finally over.

Then Esau looked up and saw Leah and Rachel and their children. "Who are all these people?" he asked.

"The Lord has blessed me very much during these last years," Jacob said. "Look, this is my family, and all these animals and servants are mine, as well. Please, take some of my donkeys and camels and sheep and goats as a gift."

"Oh no, you do not need to do that," Esau said.

"Please, Esau, they are the very least I can give you. Let me do this. It would be my joy."

Finally Esau said, yes, he would take Jacob's gifts. He invited Jacob to travel with him.

But Jacob said, because of the babies and young animals, he had to travel slowly. "Go on ahead, Esau, and we will meet you later," Jacob said.

So the two brothers said, "see you soon" and Esau went on ahead. Jacob thanked God for the peace between him and Esau.

God's Chosen People

Genesis 35:1-36:43

The night after Esau had left, when Jacob prayed to God, God answered his prayer. God said, "Go to the place where I first talked to you, to Bethel, where you had the dream about the ladder reaching up to heaven."

Jacob loaded the tents onto the camels. His sons herded the sheep, goats, donkeys and cattle, and they all headed for Bethel.

When Jacob arrived there, God appeared to him again. "Your name was Jacob, but remember, now you have a new name. You are Israel. Many of your sons and the sons of your sons will be kings. You are My chosen people," God said. From then on Jacob would be called Israel.

When he was finished praying, Israel told his family they must never worship other gods. The tribes and people around them worshipped stones and statues, the sun and the wind, instead of God Almighty.

Israel told his family to pack up for the last time. They were only a few days away from seeing his parents, Isaac and Rebekah.

When he gave the order to pack, though, he made sure Rachel did not have to lift anything. She was going to have her second baby and he wanted to take good care of her. Soon little Joseph would have a baby brother or sister.

Just after the camels were loaded, Rebekah felt the baby coming. She wanted this second baby very much. She lay down in a tent and sweated and strained. After a long while she heard someone say, "You have a boy!"

But it was too late. Rachel had worked so hard at giving life to her little boy, she lost her own. And beautiful Rachel, the love of Israel's heart, died.

Israel cried and cried. He had lost his best friend. He held the tiny baby in his arms, and his tears fell on the soft blanket. Israel called Rachel's second son Benjamin, which meant "Son of the Right Hand."

Many days later, Israel arrived back at his old home. His parents had grown very old and knew they would soon die. They had waited and waited for their son to return. When Jacob arrived, Esau was already there. Together the two sons stood by their parents as they died. Together, they buried them.

After Isaac and Rebekah's deaths, Esau said farewell to Israel. The two brothers hugged each other, friends at last. Then they went their separate ways. The promise which God had made to Esau's mother, Rebekah, when she carried Esau and Jacob in her tummy, had finally come true. Esau no longer served his younger brother. He had made a life of his own.

JOSEPH AND HIS COLORFUL ROBE
Fighting in the Tent

Genesis 37:1-:4

After Rachel and Isaac died, and Esau had moved away, Israel stayed in his parents' home and raised his twelve sons. Ten sons had Leah for a mother. Joseph and Benjamin were Rachel's sons.

Although all the boys helped their father, Joseph and Baby Benjamin were Israel's favorite sons. This made Leah's sons jealous. Israel, however, liked nothing better than to spend an afternoon playing with the baby and answering Joseph's many questions.

One day Israel was walking in a nearby market and he saw a woman who was sewing with golden needles. As she sewed a flower onto a dress, her fingers flew. She pushed the needle and colored thread through the material so fast, Israel saw only a blur where her hand had been. And when she finished, a yellow rose shone on the white cloth.

Israel had an idea. He had been meaning to buy Joseph a robe, but how much better it would be if he gave him a robe sewn by this woman and her golden needles. Israel spoke to the woman and they made a deal.

Many days later, Israel called Joseph into his tent. When Joseph arrived, he saw his father holding the beautiful robe out to him. "Here, my good son, this is for you," Israel said.

Joseph gasped in amazement. It was special to have a new robe, but to have one like this, why, he had never seen such a robe before! It was covered with bright designs, and it seemed every color of the rainbow shimmered on the cloth. Red, yellow, blue, green, they were all there. "This is a robe for a king," Joseph thought, "certainly not for me."

He said, "Oh no, Father. This is too much. This should be for you. I am only a boy, I do not deserve something as lovely as this."

"Don't be silly, Joseph. It is a gift. Of course you have not deserved it. I give it to you because I want to. Besides," Israel said with a twinkle in his eyes, "the robe is too small for me."

Joseph received the beautiful robe. But when his brothers saw his gift, they grew even more jealous than before. "Why don't we get gifts like that?" they grumbled.

Joseph's Dream

Genesis 37:5-:11

One morning, Joseph woke up with a start. He had had a very strange dream. It was so real, he felt he just had to talk to someone about it.

Joseph went looking for his brothers. "You will never guess what I dreamt last night," he said when he found them.

Joseph knew his brothers did not like him, but he loved them anyway. His mother Rachel had taught him what it meant to follow the one God, how he should be kind to others and help

whenever he saw a need. Joseph had asked God to help him not feel hurt when his brothers turned away from him. He thanked God for his brothers and prayed they could all learn to be best friends some day.

Even though his brothers were mean, Joseph was so excited by his dream, he hardly noticed. He said, "I had a strange dream. We were all out in the field, tying the grain into bundles. Suddenly, my bundle stood straight up, while all your bundles came and stood in a circle around mine and bowed down to it."

His brothers pretended not to listen, but Joseph's dreams interested them. He often dreamt funny things. This time, though, they grew angry.

"Who do you think you are? You are no king! There is no way any of us would ever bow down to you!"

A few days later Joseph had another dream. Again he told it to his brothers. "Listen," he said. "I had another dream and this time the sun and moon and eleven stars were bowing down to me." But this only made his brothers angrier.

When Joseph told his father about his dreams, Israel was stern with him, for he did not want the boy to think he was better than others.

"Do not pride yourself too much, Joseph," Israel said. Although he might have sounded serious, privately Israel took careful note of Joseph's dreams. "He is a special boy in many ways. Perhaps the dreams will be important someday," Israel thought.

In the Well

Genesis 37:12-:24

Joseph sat on the ground, rolling a ball to his baby brother. Benjamin sat opposite him, laughing and clapping his hands. When Israel saw the boys he smiled.

"They are quite a pair," he thought to himself, "no trouble at all. Still, Joseph is getting older. Perhaps he should spend more

time learning from his older brothers."

Israel said, "Joseph, I want you to follow your brothers. They have taken the sheep to pasture. See if all is well, then come back and tell me what you have learned."

Joseph jumped up and hugged his father good-bye. Then he set out. "It is a good day for an adventure," he thought. Joseph walked and walked and walked. After some time, he saw his brothers' camp just ahead.

When they saw him, though, they groaned, "Oh no, here comes that silly dreamer, Joseph. We know a way to get rid of him once and for all. Let's throw him into one of the wells near here. Then we can say a wild animal killed him. Ha! His dreams won't come true if he's dead."

"No wait," the eldest brother said. His name was Reuben. "Throw him into the well, but don't kill him. Not yet anyway." Reuben said this because he knew if he were the one to get Joseph out of the well, his father would think he was a hero. And Reuben wanted very much to be a hero.

When Joseph arrived, he panted up the last hill and smiled. He had finally found his brothers. But when he saw the looks on their faces, his smile faded. "Why are they all walking this way?" he thought. "They usually walk away from me."

His brothers formed a circle around him. He turned one way, then the other, then the other, but he was trapped. Before Joseph knew what was happening, they jumped all over him, tore off his robe and threw him into a dark, damp well.

Joseph cried out, but it did no good. Thump! He landed in the mud and looked up. All he saw were his brothers' faces laughing as they dropped sand on him. He covered his face with his hands and moved up against the slimy wall. When his brothers finally left, Joseph cried. Very quietly, he sobbed, wishing he were back home with his father and brother, playing in the sunshine.

On the Way to Egypt

Genesis 37:25-:35

That evening it was Reuben's turn to keep watch over the flocks. So he was not in camp when another brother, Judah, said to the others, "Let's not kill Joseph. I have a better idea. I saw some traders coming this way. When they get closer, let's call them over and tell them we have a slave for sale."

When the slave traders arrived, Joseph's brothers pulled him out of the well. "See how

strong he is," they said.

When they pinched him, Joseph did not cry out. He knew he was in great danger. He prayed that God would take care of him.

The traders agreed to pay twenty pieces of silver for Joseph. They strapped him onto a donkey, then rode off across the desert.

When Reuben arrived back at camp later that night, he bent over the well and whispered, "Joseph, it's all right, I'll get you out tomorrow." Reuben still planned to become a hero. But he heard no answer. "Joseph!" he called out. Silence.

"Why are you talking to an empty well?" Judah walked up behind Reuben.

"But, but, where is Joseph?" Reuben asked. Panic rose in his throat. "What have you done to our brother?" He grabbed Judah and shook him.

"Calm down," Judah said. "Here's your share." He gave two of the silver coins to Reuben.

"You sold him as a slave?" Reuben could hardly spit the words out, he was so angry.

"Yes. And by now our spoiled brother is well on his way to Egypt. It was a good idea, don't you think so?" Judah grinned.

But Reuben knew how very much Joseph meant to their father, Israel. Now instead of becoming a hero in his father's eyes, Reuben would have to break his father's heart with terrible news. Reuben decided to tell Israel that Joseph was dead. He felt he had no choice. He did not dare tell the truth.

The next day the brothers killed a goat and dipped Joseph's robe into the blood. They all went back home and showed the robe to Israel.

When Israel saw the robe, he said, "It is my son's robe! Some terrible animal has killed him. Joseph must surely be dead!"

Israel was so upset, he tore his clothes, wore rough cloth and sat in his tent, refusing to eat for many days. All he could do was cry and hold the blood-stained robe up against his face, wishing it still covered the live body of his favorite son Joseph.

JOSEPH BECOMES A SLAVE

Joseph Must Work Hard

Genesis 37:36, 39:1-:10

Joseph travelled with the slave traders a long, long way. During the first few days of the trip, Joseph had cried, feeling sorry for himself and wishing he were back home. When he ran out of tears, he started praying instead.

"Oh Lord God," he whispered as the sun beat down on him. "I don't know where I am going. It could be I will have to spend the rest of my life slaving away in the hot sun. I may have to spend all my days carrying stones so the Egyptians can make their huge pyramids. But Lord, I know wherever I am, You will be there too. Thank You. And please help me."

At night, while he tossed and turned in the sand, staring up at the stars which seemed almost close enough to touch, Joseph prayed for his family. "I think I know why my brothers did what they did. I was acting too proud. I'm sorry, Lord. Please forgive me and help them not to feel too badly. Please take special care of my brother Benjamin. And please keep Father safe so that someday I might see him again."

After many days of travelling, the traders led Joseph into a big city. They lost no time in finding a buyer for Joseph. When Joseph saw his new master, he knew God had heard his prayers and was taking care of him.

The man who bought Joseph was called Potiphar. He was rich, but more important, he was a kind man. Joseph would not have to work in the fields or haul bricks for the pyramids. Instead, he could work in Potiphar's house.

Joseph worked hard for Potiphar. He had never had to do that when he was at home. Joseph tried to find things which needed to be done before he was asked to do them. He prayed to God to help him do well.

Joseph did not feel like he was working for Potiphar, though. Instead, he felt like God was his Master. Every time he did a job, Joseph wanted it done right, so God would be pleased.

Potiphar knew Joseph was a good worker. As time went by, Potiphar put Joseph in charge of more and more. At first Joseph kept the house clean. Then he watched over work in the fields and made sure the meals were cooked right. Eventually Potiphar put Joseph in charge of everything he owned. All Potiphar had to do was decide what he wanted for dinner every night!

In Prison

Genesis 39:11-:23

While Joseph worked for Potiphar, he grew from a boy into a man. Joseph did everything well because God was blessing his efforts. Yet Joseph felt proud of himself. "After all," he thought, "I can run all of Potiphar's business."

There came a day when Potiphar's wife looked out her window and saw Joseph in the garden. "Oh, he is so handsome," she thought to herself. "My husband is gone on a trip for a few days, maybe I can get Joseph to come into my bedroom and kiss me." She called to Joseph and he came, wondering what job he might do for her.

Joseph remembered the lessons his mother Rachel had taught him. Rachel had told him there was nothing better than for a man to love a woman and have God bless the two being together.

Joseph knew many men would like to kiss Potiphar's wife. It was nice being asked to kiss a beautiful woman. But Joseph did not love her. He knew if he kissed her, it would not be fair to Potiphar, her husband and his master. Potiphar had trusted Joseph with so much. God would not be pleased if Joseph betrayed that trust.

Joseph shook his head no. "You are very beautiful," he said, "but it would not be right."

Potiphar's wife was so hurt that a slave would say "no" to her that she threw herself at Joseph, trying to force him to kiss her. When he pushed her off and ran away, she grabbed his cloak and held onto it. Oh, she was very angry and wanted to hurt Joseph, for he had made her feel like a fool.

When Potiphar came home, his wife showed him Joseph's cloak. She made up a story, "Joseph snuck into my bedroom to attack me! And you thought you could trust him. Ha! What kind of horrible man did you bring into our home?"

Potiphar believed his wife and called the guards. He was so angry he never wanted to see Joseph again. He told the guards to throw Joseph into prison. "And throw away the key!" he yelled after them as they dragged Joseph away.

But when Joseph entered her bedroom, he saw Potiphar's wife had hardly any clothes on. She just stood there.

"What is it you wanted, madam?" Joseph asked.

Potiphar's wife said, "Kiss me, Joseph. You are so good-looking and strong. I want you to kiss me."

The Dreams of Two Men

Genesis 40:1-:23

Joseph sat in the dark, damp cell all by himself. "How did I end up here?" he wondered.

The last time he had lost everything, his brothers had thrown him down the well and sold him as a slave. Joseph knew he had grown proud of his dreams and the special love his father had shown him. No wonder his brothers had been mean to him.

Now, when he asked, "Why, why, Lord, why me?" Joseph knew he had made the same mistake again. He had been too proud of all the jobs he did for Potiphar. He had even been proud of saying no to Potiphar's wife. Yet that was nothing to be proud of. That was just doing right. All the jobs he had done so well, that had been because of God's blessing, not because Joseph was so good.

Joseph bowed his head in shame. "I'm sorry, Lord. I've done it again. Please forgive me and please help me to change."

One morning two prisoners came to Joseph with a problem. "We had terrible dreams last night. Can you tell us what they mean?"

Joseph said, "I cannot help you, but my God may tell me what they mean so I can help you."

The first man, who used to carry Pharaoh's cup and make sure it was always full of wine, described his dream. "I saw a vine, and on the vine were three branches. As soon as the branches had little flowers on them, the blossoms became grapes. Pharaoh's cup was in my hand, and I took the grapes, squeezed them into Pharaoh's cup and gave it to him."

Joseph said a quiet prayer, asking God for help. Then he knew the answer. "This is what your dream meant. The three branches are three days. In three days Pharaoh will say you are free. But, please," Joseph added, "could you mention me to Pharaoh and get me out of this prison?"

The second man had been Pharaoh's chief baker. He told Joseph his dream. "On my head were three baskets of bread. In the top basket was bread for Pharaoh. Then birds landed on me and ate the bread which was meant for Pharaoh."

Joseph hesitated. God had shown him what the dream meant and it was not nice. "The three baskets are three days. This is not good news. In three days' time Pharaoh will cut off your head and the birds will eat your dead body."

The baker did not say a word. He just turned and went back to his cell.

Three days later, it happened exactly as Joseph had predicted. The Pharaoh's cup bearer went free and got his old job back, while the baker was killed.

The Pharaoh's Dream

Genesis 41:1-:14

Two long years went by and all that time Joseph heard nothing from Pharaoh's cup bearer. Joseph kept busy taking care of the other prisoners. He shared his food with them and scrubbed the cells. Day in and day out he saw the sunshine stream through the barred windows and he prayed God might help him be free someday.

One morning, in the palace, Pharaoh woke up screaming. All his servants came running. They saw him sitting up in bed, sweat streaming down his royal cheeks. He wiped his eyes. "It was a bad dream. But it was so real, I am sure it must mean something very important." Pharaoh looked at all the servants standing around his bed. "Don't just stand there, find someone who knows what dreams mean!" he roared at them. The servants hopped away in fright.

Then all the wizards, magicians, wise men and scientists came. They listened as Pharaoh told them about his dreams. They hummed and hawed, looked at charts, drew pictures on their scrolls, then shook their heads. No, they did not know what the dreams meant.

In the crowd around Pharaoh's bed was the royal cup bearer. He held Pharaoh's cup and made sure it stayed full of wine. It was no easy job on a day like that one, when Pharaoh was angry and frustrated that no one could help him.

The cup bearer stood listening to everyone say, no, they did not know what the dream meant, when, suddenly, he remembered a promise he had made a very long time ago. He felt terrible that he had forgotten for so long and knew it was time he spoke up.

"Pharaoh," the cup bearer said, "I made a promise to a Hebrew slave long ago, when I used to be in prison. He knew what my dream meant; he told me I would soon be freed. And I was. I promised I would mention him to you, then I forgot. But I know he could help you now. For he was also right in predicting that the baker would be killed. And you know what happened to him."

Pharaoh nodded. "That is exactly what will happen to all of you," he pointed at them, "if you cannot find someone to help me." His servants shivered as two guards ran to the prison to fetch Joseph.

Fat and Skinny Cows

Genesis 41:15-:32

When the guards dragged Joseph into Pharaoh's bedroom, all Joseph could see was a huge crowd of people. Then he saw Pharaoh, sitting up in bed and drinking wine. He bowed down.

Pharaoh said to Joseph, "I had a dream and no one can tell me what it means. Can you?"

"No, I cannot. But God may give Pharaoh an answer," Joseph said.

Pharaoh said to Joseph, "In my dream I was standing by the River Nile, when out of the river there came up seven fat cows.

They ate the grass near the river. Then seven thin and ugly cows came out of the river. I have never seen such terrible-looking cows before." Pharaoh squinted his eyes and made an ugly face as he remembered.

"The seven ugly cows ate up the seven fat cows. But when they were through eating, they still looked as thin and scrawny as before. It made no difference. The thin cows stayed thin," Pharaoh paused. He looked up at Joseph.

"But there was more. I also dreamed about seven full heads of grain, growing on a single stalk. After them seven other heads sprouted, but they were withered and thin and burned by the wind. The thin grain swallowed up the seven pieces of good grain. I told all this to the wizards, but no one could tell me what it meant." Pharaoh looked expectantly at Joseph.

Joseph stared at the ground. He prayed, "Please God, what does it all mean?" Then he

knew. Just like that, God opened Joseph's mind so he would understand what the dreams meant.

"Pharaoh, the two dreams mean the same thing. There will be seven years of plenty to eat and drink. All the poor will be fed. There will be enough food for everyone. But after those seven years will come another seven, when the crops will not grow and all the food will run out. Everyone will go hungry during those years.

"God showed Pharaoh the dream twice because He wanted you to know He has firmly decided to do this, and that it will happen soon."

Joseph swallowed hard. He knew God had wanted Pharaoh to hear these things. But there was more and he was not sure how happy Pharaoh would be to get advice from a Hebrew slave.

FamilyTime Bible Stories